The Mum in Me

Phoebe Ghorayeb

Presentation by *BookLeaf Publishing*

Web: www.bookleafpub.com

E-mail: info@bookleafpub.com

ISBN: 9789357695565

First edition 2022

This book is dedicated to my three greatest achievements.

ACKNOWLEDGEMENT

To all the people in my life who made me the mother that I am. From my own mother to my mother in law, my husband and my three children, my sisters in law, aunties, cousins, grandparents, friends and fellow mums. Thank you.

This Little Thing Called Parenting

As we lie together in the dark
And send our prayers towards the moon,
You turn your tiny face to mine
And whisper "mummy, I love you."

Suddenly my heart feels lighter
The weight on my shoulders lifted,
Who knew your words held so much power
In just one moment my whole world shifted.

Some days are pure perfection
Some days just feel unreal,
Some days I need to pinch myself,
Some days my heart, you heal.

You say your please and thank you's,
You ask politely for a toy,
With manners like the queen herself
This brings me so much joy.

As we sit and play with playdough
Or use pretend make up and do our hair,
You tell me I look beautiful
Even when my face is bare.

I love our little rituals,
Grab a coffee, go to the park,
An afternoon of baking,
Watching movies after dark.

Living room dance parties,
Playing monsters up the stairwell,
Watering your Woolies herbs,
Then at night we sing (or is it yell?)

You do as you are asked,
You don't scream or run away,
And whilst I do the cooking
You sit quietly and play.

Then somedays you help me cook
And tip the flour everywhere,
But the happiness it brings you
Means I really just don't care.

You eat up all your dinner,
You don't refuse to have a bath,
And whilst we read a bedtime story
We snuggle up and have a laugh.

We sing your favourite nursery rhymes,
Then I pass to you your teddy
And as I creep out through the door,
You whisper, "missing you already".

Sometimes it's days like this
That don't happen all too often,
In amongst the struggles
They are easily forgotten.

But their rarity is what makes them special
That remind us why we do,
This little thing called parenting
Because there's no one else like you.

So as we gaze towards the ceiling
That's dancing with your nightlights stars,
I'll take the good days with the bad
Because they're nobody's but ours.

Your Imagination Is GOAT

Fingernails made of felt tip lids,
Tattoos made of stickers,
A Pearl bracelet cut from a piece of paper,
A hat fashioned from knickers.

A glittering scarf that mimics hair,
And makes an excellent top and skirt,
A pipe cleaner is the perfect pet,
And a tent using dads work shirt.

A microphone using a hairbrush,
A sofa becomes a boat,
Stacks of pillows make a cubby den,
Your imagination is GOAT.

To be inside your mind,
To see the chaos that unfolds,
To be a witness to your dreams,
To see the magic that's untold.

What I wouldn't give,
To see the world through younger eyes,
And to finally realise,
The adult world is in fact lies.

My Darling, Mi Amor

Your tear is like a shard of glass
And it cuts me to my core,
As I watch it trickle down your cheek
And drip off your tiny jaw.

Your tears move in slow motion,
Your face crinkles up in pain,
I see the sadness in your eyes,
The blood from your face drains.

You look at me like I let you down
And it's this that hurts me more.
I'm supposed to protect you.
My darling, mi amor.

You're innocent and confused,
Why is the world so mean?
It doesn't understand you,
Why do you feel unseen?

I'm trying to explain to you
But you just can't comprehend.
I try to hug and hold and kiss you
But your screams drown out my zen.

There's nothing that I wouldn't do,
To take your pain away.
I'd rather hurt a million times,
Than see you hurt for just one day.

And then your cries turn to whimpers
And your breathing slowly calms.
You snuggle up against my chest
And put your palm into my palm.

And for a moment the world stops turning
And it's just you and me,
Our heartbeats sing in unison,
The pain is gone, you're free.

Fuck It

I love being a mummy
There's no doubt about it.
But love doesn't always mean like
And sometimes I think...f&*k it.

You can watch the iPad and TV
During breakfast, lunch and supper.
It's 9am and I'm already struggling,
So it's CBeebies turn to mother.

Weetbix, toast and scrambled eggs
It's an all day breakfast for you.
Cooking today? I just can't be arsed,
As long as you're full it'll do.

30 minutes of exercise
Is the daily recommendation.
Well yelling and screaming sure builds up a
sweat,
Feels like my mouth just ran a marathon.

Right then kids, time to get arty
Here's some paper and some glue.
Stick it, rip it, tear it to shreds,
It ain't no Picasso but hey, it'll do.

Now for some literature
What book shall we read?
Surprise, surprise that one again.
Please don't mind me if I fall asleep.

So it's just hit midday
And we still haven't got dressed
But the idea of clothing
Feels like the ultimate test.

I'm skipping your bath
A quick wipe down will suffice
Then I'll smother you in lotion
So at least you'll smell nice.

Cleaning the house?
That's been the last thing on my mind.
My day has been consumed
With merely keeping kids alive.

Take some time for me they say
That's easier said than done.
I spend most of the day chasing my tale,
Wearing sweats and a 5 day old mum bun.

Somedays are a shocker
Somedays I'm just not cut out.
But no matter how much I fail,
I will always love you no doubt.

Somedays I'm nailing this shit
Somedays I feel like an amateur.
Somedays I just want to start again,
Everyday as a parent sure is an adventure.

There is no manual or guide book
Your instinct is your power.
Always remember you're a mum for a reason,
And some things take time to flower.

I wouldn't change it for the world
Because you are my world you see.
And I assure that I'll never give up,
Because without you, there is no me.

Somedays I Am Mum

Somedays I will smile,
Somedays I will shout,
Somedays I will win,
Somedays I will tap out.

Somedays I will feel low,
Somedays I'm on a high,
Somedays I will laugh,
Somedays I will cry.

Somedays I will hide,
Somedays I feel elated,
Somedays I will sing,
Somedays I feel deflated.

Somedays I will sigh,
Somedays I will moan,
Somedays I will wince,
Somedays I will groan.

Somedays I will triumph,
Somedays I'll punch the sky,
Somedays I will surprise myself,
Somedays I will high five.

Somedays I am mama,
Somedays I am mum,
Somedays I am mummy,
Somedays I am...................
muuuuuuuuuuuuuum!!!!!!

But whatever day it is
And however I may feel,
Being your mum is a privilege
And it's because of you, I have found me.

5:30am

It's 5:30am
And I am awake.
Why am I awake?
My kids are awake.

It's early
I am tired.
Like, really tired.
But I'm awake now.

I look outside
And see the sky.
The sky is pink,
Like sherbet.

I stare in awe
At it's beauty
And I'm at peace
With being awake.

Because of them,
My kids,
I get to witness
This thing if beauty.

They open my eyes.
Literally.
But also figuratively
Because of them I see.

I see things I didn't believe,
Things I didn't know,
Things I couldn't imagine.
I see because they see.

The sky is blushing
My heart is full.
It's 5:30am
And I am awake.

Zaki

My baby boy, my precious son,
How proud I am to be your mum.
But since I was young I do remember,
Girls were always on my agenda.

I'd brush their hair and play with dolls,
Watch Frozen, Little Mermaid and Trolls.
Decorate cupcakes with all things sparkling,
Practice our catwalk, singing and dancing.

I didn't want to kick a ball,
Or climb a tree and take the fall.
Playing with Batman and toy guns,
Didn't sound like all that fun.

But that's not what a boy's about,
And now you're here I realise that.
You are more than just a boy my love,
There's a reason you were sent from above.

It's true what they say about a mother and son,
A connection that cannot be outdone.
I love my girls, it's plain to see,
But you complete us, our little Zaki.

Not Goodbye

Life, for the most part, is beautiful,
Oh how lucky we are,
To be given a shot at existence,
To be plucked from a billion stars.

Life is also quite funny,
You see there's a price we must pay,
As great as this gift is we're given,
Eventually there comes a day.

When we're faced with our own mortality
And reminded how fragile we are,
The clock will one day stop ticking
And we're put back to live with the stars.

I used to be scared of dying
All the adventures I would miss,
All the milestones I'd miss out on,
All the people I'd no longer kiss.

I'm still afraid of dying
Although it's no longer about me,
To leave my children without a mother,
What kind of mother would that make me?

To think of how sad they would be
Is the thing that hurts me the most.
To witness their life from afar,
Nothing more than an invisible ghost.

But that day is not today,
With a billion more beats to go,
My heart will find the strength,
To be with you for every tomorrow.

Not The Perfect Parent

I'm sorry if I mess this up,
For the times I get it wrong,
I'm learning on this journey,
Sometimes the road feels long.

I don't think I will ever know,
How I'm meant to do this,
With a constant moving target,
It's no surprise I'll often miss.

I'm not the perfect parent,
Nor will I ever be,
There will be times I'll make you cry,
I hope you can forgive me?

And everyone seems to think,
That for you they know what's best,
They watch and point the finger,
Like I'm a sitting a parental test.

As well as being a parent,
I am also just a human,
I get tired and angry and sad,
But I am doing the best I can.

And as long as you three know,
That I'll try with all my soul,
To give you the best of me,
Because my heart you stole.

Battleground

Today was not a good one,
Neither of us won.
You kicked and screamed and tantrumed.
And I sucked out all the fun.

My patience was running thin,
You pushed and pushed and pushed.
As my temper with you rose,
I shushed and shushed and shushed.

I immersed myself in housework
Just so I had a reason,
Not to sit and play with you
It felt like parental treason.

My energy was dwindling
While yours was running high.
I didn't want to parent
All I wanted was to cry.

I felt lost, I felt confused
I'm meant to be the strong one,
To hold you when you crumble
But today I was outdone.

Am I failing as a mother
If I just don't want to be,
Every minute of everyday
In my children's company?

Somedays are a battleground,
Somedays are a wall,
My stubbornness is my demise
But if I fall, you fall.

It wasn't easy for either of us
But at least I understand,
That with the bad days come the good
If we face them hand in hand.

I know that we will have
Many more days just like this,
But so long as we remember
To end each one with a kiss

Punching Bag

When you tell me you don't like me,
A little part of me feels lost.
When you refuse to cuddle up to me,
I fight back tears at all cost.

When you say that you love daddy more,
I wonder what I did to fail?
You make me feel like second best,
My colour drains and I turn pale.

When you ask for him to tuck you in,
My heart fills with jealousy.
It's me who tended to you all day,
Who hugged you when you scraped your knee.

I know that you are growing
And understanding how you feel.
I try not to take it personally,
But what you say sometimes feels real.

It's hard to be the punching bag
But you know I'll never fight back.
I'll happily take the hits
And try not to show the cracks.

And then you say the dreaded word,
It begins with H and ends in E.
They say words will never hurt
But this one cut right through me.

You yell at me to go away,
You tell me to not touch you.
But all I want to do right now,
Is hug and kiss and love you.

So much power in someone so small,
Of which I am here to guide.
When you throw at me your daggers,
I will refuse to run and hide.

And then you say my favourite word,
It begins with L and ends in E.
And I'm reminded once again,
No matter what, it's you and me.

Thank You Mr G

There's not much in this world
That your dad cannot do.
A man of many skills and talents
That have always seen him through.

But his biggest skill, his biggest gift,
His biggest achievement by far
Is a little one called fatherhood
And man, he's set the bar.

He shows his love not just with words
But with hugs and gestures and time.
His love is our family's superglue,
He's our backbone, our spine.

His obsession with his children
Is the purest I have seen.
He cannot live without them
They are the oxygen he breathes.

Being a daddy suits him
I can't remember him before.
His girls have now completed him,
He's a dada down to his core.

V and S will never know
Just how blessed they are.
He is all their hopes and wishes come true,
He is their lucky star.

So on behalf of them
I say thank you Mr G,
For being more than we imagined,
For being the daddy of their dreams.

Body, I'm sorry

I love my body,
Most of the time.
But it's not always easy,
To try to be kind.

When I was younger
I would pull it apart,
Poke it and prod it,
This was just the start.

I was modelling more,
I was eating less,
My urge to purge,
Wear a size 0 dress.

Counting calories,
Counting steps,
Counting intake,
Counting reps.

I tortured myself
From the outside in,
Measuring my worth,
Against a need to be thin.

Seven years go by,
What a journey it's been,
But my body's great challenge
Was about to be seen.

Falling pregnant with you
Was my happiest day,
And the changes ahead
Would put my demons at bay.

The biggest I'd been
But my most content yet,
I could enjoy food
And no longer fret.

I realised my body
Was more than a mannequin,
It's purpose in life,
Was to hold you within.

Then when you arrived,
I was squishy and floppy,
But I didn't care,
I was finally happy.

To my body I'm sorry,
For the years of abuse,
You did not deserve it,
Let's call a truce.

Still my body's not perfect,
It never has been,
Or was it?
It was just never seen.

To this day I still struggle,
Maybe that's just how it goes,
But I'm learning to love me,
From my head to my toes.

And if not for me,
For my awesome three kiddy's,
Because to me you are perfect,
My Valentina, Siddy and Zaki.

Mumstagram Vs Reality

It's easy to see perfection,
In another mother's day,
But you don't see behind closed doors,
She probably thinks the same.

Why don't I dress like that?
Why don't I have it figured out?
Why don't I cook that food?
Why am I constantly in doubt?

Our children are our greatest gift,
And we want for them the best,
But comparison can make us feel,
Like we failed the parental test.

"They" say don't compare yourself
To other mamas on the grid,
This can be easier said than done,
When "real life" is one big fib.

You see organic, homemade food,
Kids dressed in the latest trends,
You see a care fee family holiday,
The jealously builds, you can't pretend.

You continue to scroll,
Then you scroll a little more,
You've hit the downward spiral,
Into the deepest, darkest hole.

And then you start to question,
What is your life's purpose?
Needing to showcase to the world,
To prove you are not worthless.

It's hard, I know it's hard,
Somedays I need to be reminded,
That social media's not real life,
And we can be easily blindsided.

If you think a mum is doing well,
Then take from her a tip,
Instead of feeling like you don't stack up,
Then saddle up and crack the whip.

Celebrate your fellow mums,
But most importantly celebrate you,
Yes other mums are wonderful,
But so are you, it's true!

Mother In Law

The mother in law,
The evil witch,
The dragon lady,
The ultimate bitch.

Because of Disney,
We're made to think,
That a mother in law,
Should down right stink.

When I tell my friends,
She's staying with us,
They heave a sigh,
And begin to cuss.

You're brave they say,
Or are you crazy?
I shrug my shoulders,
"She doesn't faze me."

In fact, I like her,
Is that so odd?
They stare at me,
And slowly nod.

But nobody
Seems to know,
That our relationship,
Is friend not foe.

She scooped me up,
Under her wing,
Like one of her own,
She took me in.

How lucky am I,
That she fits like a glove?
Because actually like,
Is more like love.

The Cure

They say motherhood is life changing,
I think I can top it,
I recently had heart surgery,
I know? Who'd have thought it.

I had a 4 year old, a 3 year old,
I had also just had a baby,
But between you and me I believe,
He was the one that saved me.

I lived to 34 not knowing,
That my heart was a little obscure,
And it was whilst I was 30 weeks pregnant,
We discovered I needed a cure.

And so all the testing began,
Appointments here and there,
And two months after giving birth,
I was admitted to cardio care.

I spent six hours under the knife,
As they pieced me back to new,
Two holes to fix and valves to mend,
Followed by eight long days in ICU.

And after that came medication,
And rehab twice a week,
They told me it'd be 3 long months,
Until I reached my peak.

As I write this I'll let you know,
I'm six weeks post operation,
It's had its challenges I cannot lie,
But I brought with me determination.

As well as finding strength within,
I must give thanks to my family,
Because of them, because of their love,
I believe it's them who ultimately cured me.

To The Mums

To the mums hanging at the park
I see you
To the mums wide awake in the dark
I see you

To the mums in constant disarray
I see you
To the mums who run around all day
I see you

To the mums who are the 24/7 chauffeur
I see you
To the mums who rudely get called "her"
I see you

To the mums preparing the 11th meal of the day
I see you
To the mums washing up and putting away
I see you

To the mums having a tough time
I see you
To the mums whose kids turn on a dime
I see you

To the mums constantly on repeat
I see you
To the mums sacrificing opportunities to eat
I see you

To the mums with little time alone
I see you
To the mums turning houses homes
I see you

To the mums who feel unseen
I see you
And even when it doesn't feel it
Your children see you too

My Greatest Title

What a gift,
What an honour,
To be your world,
To be your mother.

My greatest title,
My greatest role,
It has its highs,
It takes its toll.

Some days are hard,
Some days are gold,
This never stops….
So I've been told.

I love the journey,
I love the adventure.
Full of surprises,
Full of wonder.

Life before?
I can't remember,
You are now,
My new forever.

Blessed am I
In every way,
Every second, every minute
......Everyday